How to Dress Like a
PRINCESS
The Secrets of Kate's Wardrobe

Splendid
PUBLICATIONS

Claudia Joseph

SILVER LADY: KATE WEARS JENNY PACKHAM AT THE INAUGURAL TUSK CONSERVATION AWARDS, IN 2013; FOR HER FIRST OFFICIAL EVENING ENGAGEMENT, THE ARK GALA, IN 2011; AND AT THE 2015 SPECTRE PREMIERE.

How to Dress Like a Princess:
The Secrets of Kate's Wardrobe

Claudia Joseph

Splendid Publications Ltd
Unit 7
Twin Bridges Business Park
South Croydon
Surrey
CR2 6PL

www.splendidpublications.co.uk

British Library Cataloguing in Publication Data is available from The British Library

ISBN: 9781909109728

Designed by BatDesign, Lucy Hobbs and Thomas Sammut

Jacket designed by Chris Fulcher

Drawings by Tanya Bennett

Commissioned by Shoba Vazirani

Printed by PPG, Portsmouth

BLOOMING IN BLUE: KATE WEARS MAX MARA FOR A 2013 VISIT TO HOPE HOUSE.

PRETTY IN PINK: KATE WEARS A PALE PINK ALEXANDER MCQUEEN COAT AND JANE TAYLOR HAT FOR THE 2015 COMMONWEALTH DAY SERVICE.

Contents

To my favourite fashionistas: Johanna and Victoria

BLACK BEAUTY: IN TEMPERLEY LONDON AND LOCK & CO FOR THE 2013 REMEMBRANCE DAY SERVICE.

Introduction

She is a global fashion phenomenon:
from the moment she became engaged to
Prince William, thousands of copy
Kates scoured the Internet to find out where
she had bought her Royal blue Issa dress.
Since then the Duchess of Cambridge has
been responsible for phones ringing off
the hook and websites crashing as fans try
to emulate her regal look. She is credited
with a £1 billion boost in the economy and
appeared in Time magazine's top 100 Most
Influential People in the World. Now you
can discover the secrets of Kate's wardrobe.
Whether you want to choose an outfit for
Ascot or wellies for the Beauleigh Horse
Trials, this unique guide to dressing for
the Social Season is the book for you. As
you scroll through its pages, you will get a
glimpse inside Kate's make-up bag; find
out the parallels between The Queen and
her grand-daughter-in-law; discover the
Duchess's favourite clothing; and marvel at
her £600,000 jewellery collection.

The Secrets of Kate's Wardrobe

Kate in Numbers

If she had taken a different career path, the Duchess of Cambridge could have been a supermodel - whether she is walking down the catwalk at St Andrews University or mingling with the stars in Tinseltown, she looks sensational. Carole White, who co-founded the model agency Premier, estimates that Kate, who is five feet ten inches tall, measures 32-24-35 - the same size as her namesake Kate Moss. That makes her a UK size eight. 'With those measurements and her height, Kate definitely could be a model,' she said.

Kate in Colours

Kate's favourite colour is blue - according to Vogue. The magazine did a Katepedia of her wardrobe and discovered that - in the first two years of her marriage - she wore shades of blue 24 per cent of the time. But even the Duchess has been known to get it wrong. Perhaps she should join the Mumsnet crowd and 'get her colours done'.

10/10...vibrant enough to give her a glow without being distracting

3/10
...too dark and wears Kate

FOUR COLOURS BLUE (L-R): IN A MADDERSON DRESS FOR THE OPENING OF THE CLORE ART ROOM; AN LK BENNETT DRESS AT NORTHOLT HIGH SCHOOL; A SERAPHINE COAT AT THE KENSINGTON ALDRIDGE ACADEMY; IN EMILIA WICKSTEAD AT THE NATIONAL PORTRAIT GALLERY.

8/10...makes her complexion look even toned

Analyst Melissa Nicholson believes that Kate best suits a summer palette, which means she looks better in clothes that have a cool blue tint rather than a warm yellow one. 'It is quite obvious that Kate is a summer,' she says. 'I would say her best shades are French navy, air force blue, aubergine, plum, burgundy, soft berry and grey (anything from silver to slate).

'Spring colours are too bright and playful for Kate, winter colours too overpowering and autumn colours are too heavy and boring. The summer colours accentuate her natural beauty – she looks sophisticated and elegant in cool soft tones.'

7/10

...dusky pastel makes her look healthy.

In the Queue

When she was first married, the Duchess of Cambridge was often spotted browsing in Kensington or Chelsea: she would pop into stores unannounced - while her security guard waited outside the door - and queue for the tills with other customers as she did before her wedding. But now she prefers to shop in the luxury of her own home. She stopped shopping in person after a group of fans followed her into a shop and hassled her - they didn't take the hint, even when she politely asked them for privacy. So that spelled the end of her shopping trips.

The Look Book

As Kate is at the top of every designer's wish list, they send Look Books for the Autumn/ Winter and Spring/Summer collections to Kensington Palace to allow her to peruse the photographs and fabric swatches at her leisure.

A few weeks later, Kate's personal assistant will call each designer asking them to send round roughly half a dozen outfits for her to try on. There is often a pile of bags at the policeman's box on the gates of Kensington Palace for her perusal.

The Duchess usually takes pieces 'on approval'. She removes each piece from the packaging and tries it on before respectfully folding and repackaging it (or her assistant does). No reason is given for their return. So you could be wearing a piece of clothing which has been tried on by our future Queen.

A Priceless Signature

Kate does not inform the designers when – or if – she will be wearing their outfits. That ensures that she maintains the wow factor when she steps out in public. She only pays once she has worn them. Her office calls the respective store to ask for an invoice and the Duchess pays promptly with a personal cheque.

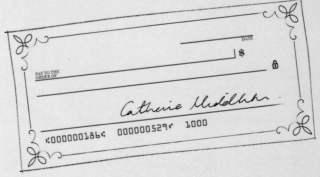

The Royal Wallet

Prince Charles meets the cost of Kate's clothing for official functions and engagements from his revenue from the Duchy of Cornwall while Prince William - who inherited £10 million from his late mother Princess Diana's estate when he turned 30 - pays for her mufti from his private fortune. Even her mother Carole Middleton chips in: she regularly buys clothes and accessories for Kate out of her own pocket. Rumours that The Queen is displeased with her expenditure are far off the mark - courtiers insist her wardrobe is 'extraordinary value for money'.

Freebies

Kate's seal of approval is like gold dust – the publicity can make a designer's name so bags of clothes arrive at Kensington Palace daily. However, the Duchess of Cambridge cannot accept freebies – they are swiftly returned with a polite note from her personal secretary. That does not mean Kate does not like a bargain. She is just as happy shopping at Bicester Village shopping outlet.

The Labels

Designers' Dream

As well as buying off the peg, the Duchess commissions couturiers such as Alexander McQueen, Alice Temperley, Catherine Walker and Jenny Packham to design for her. They have to sign draconian confidentiality agreements with Kensington Palace to stop them revealing Kate's fashion secrets. The Duchess is more secretive than The Queen.

Diplomatic Duchess

Kate champions British designers when overseas but cleverly makes a passing nod to her hosts. On her first day in Canada, she chose a dress by Montreal-born designer Erdem Moralioğlu; in the United States she chose American Diane von Furstenberg's Maja dress while on tour of Singapore she wore a printed dress designed by Singapore-born Prabal Gurung.

HIGH STREET HOTTIE: THIS ZARA MINIDRESS SOLD OUT WITHIN AN HOUR AFTER KATE WORE IT TO THE ALBERT HALL IN 2011.

CHAMPIONING NEW LABELS: KATE BLOOMS IN A TOPSHOP DRESS AND GOAT COAT DURING A VISIT TO CHILD BEREAVEMENT UK IN 2013.

High Street Hottie

While British designers are clamouring to dress the Duchess, it is the High Street where she is most at home – French Connection, Hobbs, LK Bennett, Reiss, Topshop, Warehouse, Whistles and Zara are all staples of her wardrobe. For her official engagement shoot with Mario Testino, she shunned posh labels for Reiss's £159 Nanette dress and Whistles's £95 Amy blouse – renamed the Kate. She went on honeymoon in a £49.99 cornflower blue Zara frock – and when she met the Obamas, she outshone the First Lady in Reiss's £175 beige Shola shift.

Champion of New Labels

For new designers such as Beulah, Goat and Libélula, Kate's seal of approval can make or break them. When she wore a scarlet gown by Beulah to a ball at St James' Palace in October 2011, it put the ethical label, which donates a portion of its profits to victims of India's sex trafficking trade, on the map. 'I think I screamed the first time I found out that the Duchess had chosen to wear one of our dresses,' said owner Lady Natasha Rufus Isaacs. 'We were a relatively unknown and young label, and it definitely helped spread the word about us.'

Sole Secrets

Have you ever wondered how Kate manages to walk around all day in skyscraper heels - and not get blisters or bunions? She has discovered one of the fashion industry's best-kept secrets: Alice Bow insoles. Shoe maker Rachel Bowditch created the £14.95 leather insoles, which come in a selection of colours fit for a princess, including silver, gold, rose gold and bronze. 'All I wanted was to be comfortable in my favourite shoes,' she said. 'But I couldn't bear to put unsightly insoles into my prize possessions in case anyone saw them when I slipped them off. So I started to make my own.'

A Fashion Queen

STYLE ICON: KATE WAS INSPIRED BY GRACE KELLY WHEN SHE CHOSE HER WEDDING DRESS.

Style Icon

It was a visit to the Victoria and Albert Museum's 2010 exhibition 'Grace Kelly - Style Icon' that is believed to have inspired Kate's wedding gown. Certainly her frock bore more than a passing similarity to the lace creation that the Hollywood actress wore for her 1956 wedding to Prince Rainier of Monaco. And she looked just as beautiful.

Cover Girl

Kate has had a major impact on British fashion since she married Prince William and has been selected by Time magazine as one of their Most Influential People in the World. She has topped the best-dressed lists at Vanity Fair magazine three times and has been cover girl of Vogue and Vanity Fair, as well as winning numerous awards for her sense of style...

Awards

2006 Daily Telegraph - Most Promising Newcomer

2007 Tatler - Top Ten Style Icon

2007 People magazine - Best Dressed List

2007 Richard Blackwell - Top Ten Fabulous Fashion
Independents

2008 Style.com - Monthly Beauty Icon

2008 Vanity Fair - International Best Dressed List

2010 People magazine - Best Dressed List

2010 Vanity Fair - Best Dressed List

2011 Harpers Bazaar - Queen of Style

2011 Vanity Fair - Best Dressed List

2011 Global Language Monitor - Top Fashion Buzzword

2012 Vanity Fair - Best Dressed List

2012 Vanity Fair - Cover star

2012 Headwear Association - Hat Person of the Year

2012 Time magazine – List of 100 most influential people
in the world

2013 Vanity Fair - Best Dressed List

2013 Time magazine - List of 100 most influential people in
the world

2016 Vogue magazine - Cover star

The Kate Effect

The Engagement Dress

One day she was plain Kate Middleton.
The next she was engaged to a future King.
Overnight she became a global fashion
phenomenon. Phones rang, websites crashed
and chat rooms went into meltdown as hordes
of copy Kates - desperate to emulate their idol -
descended on Harvey Nichols to buy her Royal
blue Issa engagement dress (even a £16
knock-off version at Tesco sold out within an
hour of going online).

The Engagement Photographs

So when did the Kate Effect strike again? When
she and Prince William released their official
engagement photographs taken by Princess
Diana's favourite snapper Mario Testino (he
photographed her for the cover of Vogue). In
one photograph she wore Reiss's £159 Nanette
gown. Immediately their website went into
meltdown and crashed for two hours. Reiss
re-released the dress – only for it to sell out
again – so customers were forced to bid on eBay
if they wanted to copy their icon.

One seller advertised the dress for £20 more
than it cost, writing under the description:
'Same dress worn by Kate Middleton in the
formal engagement photographs with Prince
William.' 'We have been inundated with press
coverage,' owner David Reiss said afterwards.
'At one stage, online was selling one per minute.'
Equally Whistles benefited from the goldrush.
After selling out of their £95 cream silk blouse,
they too reissued it, naming it the Kate blouse
and increasing its price to £125. 'We've had so
much publicity,' said CEO Jane Shepherdson.

Fashion Industry Boost

Market analyst Mintel estimated that Kate was
responsible for a £1 billion boost in public
spending. 'Copying Kate enables us to buy into
a little bit of her fairy-tale existence, and in
these austere times a little escapism goes a long
way,' said Mintel's senior consumer and lifestyle
analyst. 'Whether it's LK Bennett heels or a
Kate-esque blow-dry, we want a bit of her life.'

Kerching

The Kate Effect began the moment that she and Prince William got engaged. The £310 Libélula coat, which she wore to the 2011 wedding of Sarah Stourton and Harry Aubrey-Fletcher, sold out in hours and had a waiting list of 300.

London boutique Hollie de Keyser, which stocked the red Luisa Spagnoli suit Kate wore to St Andrews University, ordered 100 suits - worth £50,000 - in order to meet demand from copy Kates.

The first outfit Kate wore after the Royal Wedding - her £49.99 Zara dress and LK Bennett Greta Wedges - sold out immediately.

The Reiss website crashed after Kate wore their Shola dress for her first official engagement meeting with the Obamas. The dress promptly sold out online when service resumed.

Moloh had phone calls from around the world, offering them bribes to be bumped up the waiting list, after Kate wore their £425 Workers coat in Glasgow in 2013.

When Kate wore Diane von Furstenberg's £292 Catalina dress on her 2014 tour of Australia, it was selling on eBay within hours at £700.

The designer Sara Madderson only found out that Kate had worn their Madderson dress in 2015 when her phone rang off the hook - she did six months of online sales in 24 hours.

A fight broke out in the New York branch of Links of London between two customers fighting over their Hope Egg earrings.

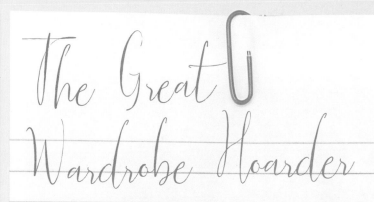

The Great Wardrobe Hoarder

So how does the Duchess try and avoid the Kate Effect? Sometimes she hoards clothes until they are seasons out of date in order to avoid causing a fashion stampede or even coming face-to-face with women in the same outfit. She waits months – or even years – before wearing purchases. So designers miss out on the boost in sales and fans are unable to copy her look – unless they pick up a bargain on eBay.

Years Old

Perhaps the oldest outfit in Kate's wardrobe is the Oasis black polo neck sweater dress that she wore underneath her Hobbs brown coat when she visited Liverpool on Valentine's Day 2012. Anyone wanting to buy the £60 figure-hugging number was sorely disappointed as Oasis revealed that it was 'years old'.

Five Years Old

However, that was not just a blip for Kate. When she visited Canada on her first Royal tour in 2011, she wore a couple of pieces which dated back five years – an Alexander McQueen white sailor dress - first worn by Sex in the City star Sarah Jessica Parker in 2006 - and a Ted Baker navy Jinan trench coat from the same year.

Four Years Old

Just months later, when she and William toured Los Angeles, Kate teamed a cream dress with a crochet top from High Street store Whistles's 2007 collection and the following March she wore Reiss's equally-old electric blue Trina number from Autumn/Winter 2008 for her first speaking engagement at the Treehouse Children's Hospice in Ipswich.

WARDROBE HOARDER: KATE IN AN ALEXANDER MCQUEEN DRESS DURING HER 2011 TOUR OF CANADA.

OUT OF DATE: WHEN KATE WORE HER JESIRÉ COAT DRESS TO THE NATIONAL PORTRAIT GALLERY IN 2012, THE LABEL HAD CEASED TRADING.

Hoarder...

Two Years Old

Even on important occasions, Kate chooses outfits from previous seasons. When she posed for her engagement photographs by Mario Testino in 2010, she wore a 2008 Whistles Amy blouse. When she accompanied The Queen and The Duchess of Cornwall to Fortnum & Mason during the Diamond Jubilee, she wore a Missoni coat dress she had bought from Bicester, dating from 2010, and when she wore her Jesiré coat dress to the National Portrait Gallery in 2012, the label was already defunct. Even when she joined the Royals for their traditional Christmas Day service at Sandringham, she chose to wrap up in Moloh's Turpin double-breasted coat, which had been in her wardrobe for two years. It was the second time that Kate had been spotted in a coat by the British brand: she wore their Workers blue and grey plaid coat on a visit to Glasgow's Emirates Arena in 2013, which dated from the previous season. Owner Caroline Smiley said: 'The Duchess is a clever shopper and often waits before she wears pieces. She's very much in control of her image and I'm sure she likes the idea things aren't still in the shops when she wears them. So not everyone can run out and buy her look.'

Months Old

Often Kate will invest in a piece one season and wear it the next. She bought her grey Reiss Angel coat from the store's Autumn/Winter 2010 collection but did not wear it until Christmas Day 2011. And she did not wear her Prabal Gurung Spring/Summer 2012 dress until that September when she went on her Singapore tour.

Team Kate

She may be married to a future King but that does not mean the Duchess of Cambridge has bowed to convention. Instead of employing a Royal dresser, she relies on a small team of trusted confidantes to help her navigate the Royal ropes - and keep her on trend.

Private Secretary

The most important member of Team Kate is Catherine Quinn, a divorced high flyer, whom the Duchess poached from Oxford University's Said Business School. The 58-year-old mother-of-one, who lives in rural Oxfordshire, is the 'gate keeper' to Kate's public AND private life. A linguist – she speaks French and German – she was Under Treasurer at Middle Temple in 2012 when William and Kate attended a fundraising dinner to mark the 600th anniversary of St Andrews University.

The Personal Assistant

Trendsetter Natasha Archer has been credited with styling the Duchess of Cambridge - but, while she acts as Kate's dresser, scouring websites for the latest trends, ordering in clothes, ironing the Royal wardrobe and dragging around her wheelie suitcase, Kate makes her own choices. Tash, as she is known, went to Uppingham boarding school, then read Hispanic Studies at King's College, London University. She worked for the Duke and Duchess of Gloucester before joining the Royal Household in 2007. In 2017 she married Royal photographer Chris Jackson in a medieval French mansion near Bordeaux.

The Fashion Editor

Just like Princess Diana, Kate's first port of call when choosing her wedding dress designer was Vogue magazine. But, unlike the 19-year-old Diana, Kate, then 28, knew her own mind. She ultimately chose the same designer as her stepbrother-in-law's wife Sarah Buys, a fashion editor who also wore Alexander McQueen on her wedding day. Vogue Editor Alexandra Shulman, who drew up a list of designers with Sarah Burton at the top, said: 'I think she was very determined to choose who she wanted, no matter who had suggested what. She was going to make her own decision - that was absolutely clear. I was really pleased and thrilled as I think it was a brave choice to make.'

TRENDSETTER: PA NATASHA ARCHER ACTS AS KATE'S UNOFFICIAL DRESSER.

Crowning Beauty

Whether she wears her hair down, in an Alice band, half-up and half-down or in a chignon, Kate's tresses are the envy of women worldwide. In fact, according to Google, the second most searched-for question about Kate is: 'Who does the Duchess of Cambridge's hair?' But, according to her husband, her lustrous locks are a 'nightmare' to style. So, who has the dubious honour of looking after her crowning beauty?

QUEEN OF CRIMPERS: HAIRDRESSER AMANDA COOK
TUCKER IS THE DUCHESS'S STYLIST ON ROYAL TOURS.

The Queen of Crimpers

The most important woman in Kate's armoury is hairdresser Amanda Cook Tucker. A trusted confidante, Mandy is Kate's stylist on Royal tours. She and ex-husband Neville Tucker, who trained crimper Richard Ward, have mingled in Royal circles for years. Tucker worked closely with The Queen's hairdresser Charles Martyn - his Knightsbridge salon had a Royal Warrant - while Cook Tucker cut Prince William and Prince Harry's hair as children. Her role is so crucial that she met George and Charlotte before the Middletons - or the Royals. She began styling Kate's hair in 2012 before the Royal tour of Singapore and Malaysia and was so 'indispensable' that she now accompanies her on all tours, charging £300 a day on top of expenses. First Class, of course.

The Colour King

The Duchess has her hair cut and coloured every eight weeks (with organic vegetable dye and subtle low lights) by the Middletons' favourite Richard Ward. He and protégé James Pryce - once Kate's regular stylist - created 'multiple mood boards' to come up with a demi-chignon for the Royal Wedding. Pryce went on to tend Kate's locks on her first overseas tour of Canada and America. But he lost his Royal client after he went solo, making the mistake of posting pictures of the Duchess and her hair styles on his Facebook and Twitter account. So much for Royal discretion.

The Manicurist

Before her engagement, Kate went to Peter Jones' Footopia nail spa, now off the King's Road (she had Opi's 'Privacy Please'). But on the day, she chose a 'signature manicure' from Marina Sandoval. She gave Kate a luxury hand soak, exfoliation and deep tissue massage, cut her nails into a squoval (or rounded-square) and painted them in the perfect bridal colour - a blend of Bourjois So Laque No 28 Rose Lounge and Essie's Allure No 5. The Italian cut her teeth working for fashion designer Valentino (as well as doing the shows, she did the man himself). Kate is in good hands.

The Celebrity Orthodontist

Kate's winning smile is credited to Frenchman Dr Didier Fillion, who has a surgery in London's Wimpole Street. Apparently Kate had 'micro-rotations' rather than perfect alignment to create a natural, healthy appearance rather than an artificial Hollywood smile. Fillion, who has clinics in Paris and Geneva, has also worked on the teeth of the Monaco Royal family, Kelly Brook and Sadie Frost.

The Make-Up Artist

When The Queen got married to the Duke of Edinburgh, she did her own make-up. So Kate has been following in great footsteps. She has had tips but still has not resorted to the Hollywood tradition of hiring her own make-up artist.

Inside the Royal Make-Up Bag

Flawless Skin

If you want to know the secret of Kate's flawless skin, you only have to look across the Channel to French cosmetic company Lancôme. Apparently Kate swears by their £39.50 Hydra Zen Anti-Stress Moisurising Cream and £59 Génifique Serum. She has been a fan for years of the moisturiser, which is enriched with naturally-derived plant extracts and has an SPF 15, while she carries a bottle of Génifique in her make-up bag to revive her skin after late nights and long-haul flights.

Natural Glow

You can't take the girl out of the High Street - even during Kate's beauty regime, she mixes an expensive moisturiser with a cheaper face cream. And there is no better bargain than Nivea's Pure & Natural range, which is free from parabens, silicones, colourants and mineral oils. Both Joan Collins and Victoria Beckham are fans of the brand and the Duchess has two tubs on her bathroom shelf – Nivea's £5.10 Pure & Natural Moisturising Day Cream and their £10.20 Q10 Anti-Wrinkle Night Cream. She was spotted buying the moisturisers at Boots on London's King's Road. Certainly its aloe vera and argan oil seem to be doing the trick for her English Rose complexion.

Magic Make-Up

If you want to look like the Duchess of Cambridge, you could do worse than follow in her footsteps and have a free - and highly public - make-up lesson in the beauty department of Peter Jones. Kate was a regular visitor to the Bobbi Brown counter before the Royal Wedding and was later spotted sitting on a stool being given a step-by-step tutorial on how to fill in her brows (apparently she uses a £35 Dark Brown Brow Kit). She also invested in a three-step anti-wrinkle set, which includes a £28 eye cream, a £18 corrector and a pot of tinted eye brightener for £23.50. After the Royal Wedding the company released a statement saying that one of their make-up artists had 'provided make-up artistry assistance to members of the bridal party' with a list of products to recreate Kate's look - £16.50 Eye Shadows in Ivory, Rock Star and Slate, £18 Pale Pink Blusher, £32 Pink Quartz Shimmer Brick, £18 Sandwash Pink Lipstick and £15 lip liner as well as a £14 Crystal Gloss - if you want to rush out and buy them. And don't forget their £30 Long-Wear Even Finish Foundation for a dewy base and £40 Brightening Finishing Powder, an irridescent power in shades of taupe and rose, which will give your face a glorious pearl shimmer.

Long-Wear
Even Finish Foundation
SPF 15

Luscious Lashes

Kate turns to Lancôme for the final touches of her make-up - heavy eyeliner, smoky eyes and long lashes. She loves their £23 Artliner, which promises never to smudge, and £24.50 Hypnôse Mascara, a foam-tipped liquid liner for precise application. Kate stocks up at Peter Jones but it is not the only department store which stocks the brand if you want to copy her signature look. Lancôme's Head of Elite Team Shehla Shaikh said: 'The Duchess of Cambridge's look is classic and elegant with a daytime smoky eye. Starting with fresh matte skin, the eyes are smudged softly with a charcoal shadow to add softness. Then the top and bottom lash line are defined with a liquid liner (this could be achieved by Lancôme Artliner) and several coats of black mascara (this could be achieved by Lancôme Hypnôse mascara). Freshness is added with a rose pink blush on the apple of the cheeks and matching lips to balance the whole look.'

Beauty Secrets

No make-up bag is complete without YSL's £25 Touche Éclat - like models, actresses and popstars, the Duchess has a YSL miracle click-pen concealer in her handbag. One flies off the shelves every ten seconds - not bad for a brand, which was launched when Kate was still a gawky pupil at primary school.

Finishing Touches

When the Duchess of Cambridge wanted a scent for the Royal Wedding, she turned to Illuminum perfumier Michael Boadi, who created her favourite White Gardenia Petals fragrance. Now the small independent artisan company is pulling out all the stops to cope with demand. Illumimum describes the £125 scent, which has base notes of Precious Woods, middle notes of Gardenia, YlangYlang and Jasmine and top notes of Bergamot, Cassis and Lily as 'a delicate, refined scent'. 'The top note of lily evokes summer ambiance, whilst heart notes of gardenia, ylang ylang and jasmine are sumptuous and feminine. Amber wood underscores this light bouquet.'

Parallels with The Queen

The Queen of Green

REGAL IN RED: A VISIT TO NEWMARKET
ANIMAL HEALTH TRUST IN 2009.

One is the world's richest woman, who is descended from generations of Royalty; the other is a commoner who married into the Royal family. Yet The Queen and the Duchess of Cambridge are cut from the same cloth: they both want to get the most out of their wardrobes by wearing clothes again and again - and recycling them to their nearest and dearest. They even share a preference for the colour blue.

FOUR YEARS LATER: LEAVING KING EDWARD
VII HOSPITAL AFTER A STOMACH AILMENT.

ROYAL BLUE: VISIT TO SCOTLAND'S GOLDEN JUBILEE HOSPITAL IN 2008.

Her Majesty was brought up in wartime Britain, during an age of austerity. She famously had to collect ration coupons for her wedding dress. Frugal by nature, she comes from a generation which learnt to make do and mend - she is known for going around turning off Palace lights and insisting that shredded newspaper, rather than straw, is used in the stables. So it is barely surprising that she is willing to dust down her garments and wear them over and over again.

BACK AGAIN: ON A TRIP TO GLOUCESTER IN 2009.

The Princess of Thrift

Kate is the scion of a family of impoverished miners, whose family gentrified over the centuries, and she wants to make the most of her wardrobe. So it is fitting that The Queen of Green is Kate's biggest inspiration.She echoes her thrift by dressing for less - shopping in High Street stores and buying designer labels from Bicester Village shopping outlet.

GRACEFUL IN GREY: IN ORLA KIELY AT DULWICH PICTURE GALLERY IN 2012.

BACK AGAIN: ON A VISIT TO CHANCE UK THREE YEARS LATER.

TWICE IN A YEAR: A JENNY PACKHAM GOWN FOR A 2014
VISIT TO LONDON'S NATIONAL PORTRAIT GALLERY.

It is there that she snapped up her Missoni coat dress that she wore to Fortnum & Mason with The Queen and Duchess of Cornwall. She is even known to wear the same outfit twice in a week - she was snapped in an Emilia Wickstead dress at the Sovereign's lunch at Windsor Castle in 2012 AND at her first garden party at Buckingham Palace. Top marks for thrifty Kate.

ACROSS THE ATLANIC: AT NEW YORK'S METROPOLITAN
MUSEUM OF ART.

The Queen of Recycling

The Queen has one of the most extensive wardrobes in the world - but that does not mean she is averse to sharing. She used to pass on her hand-me-downs to senior staff, some of whom sold them through dress agencies (they were caught out when a TV mini-series bought some to clothe their screen Queen).

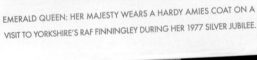

EMERALD QUEEN: HER MAJESTY WEARS A HARDY AMIES COAT ON A VISIT TO YORKSHIRE'S RAF FINNINGLEY DURING HER 1977 SILVER JUBILEE.

ON THE BALCONY: PRINCESS MARGARET TEAMS HER SISTER'S COAT WITH A WHITE HAT TO COMMEMORATE VE DAY IN 1995.

LOOKING SERENE: IN ANOTHER HARDY AMIES COAT FOR THE 1977 STATE OPENING OF PARLIAMENT.

And, when Princess Margaret was still alive, the two petite sisters - Margaret was three inches shorter than her Majesty - were often snapped sharing outfits. However, while The Queen chose discreet accessories, Margaret was more flamboyant.

TROOPING THE COLOUR: PRINCESS MARGARET ON HER WAY TO THE 1995 CEREMONY.

The Princess of Generosity

LUCKY DRESS: KATE WEARS THIS ISSA DRESS AT WIMBLEDON IN 2008.

RED AND WHITE: PIPPA TEAMS THE SAME DRESS WITH RED PUMPS THREE YEARS LATER.

FIRST OUTING: KATE CARRIES A WILBUR & GUSSIE GOLD CLUTCH
BAG FOR THE 100 WOMEN IN HEDGE FUNDS GALA IN 2011.

Where The Queen leads, Kate follows. So it is no surprise that a heap of clothes swapping goes on between the Duchess of Cambridge and her sister Pippa. They raid each other's wardrobes as the mood takes them - and swap garments regularly.

IN THE RED: PIPPA BORROWS THE BAG FOR THAT YEAR'S
BOODLES BOXING BALL.

Kate's Favourites

♡

Favourite Coats

'The Duchess is an inspiration. She's very graceful, gracious and she's a brilliant ambassador for British fashion. She mixes up designer and High Street: the perfect modern-day woman.'
- Alice Temperley

Day by Birger et Mikkelsen Brocade Coat

When Kate has something to celebrate, she invariably pulls out this champagne brocade coat by Day Birger et Mikkelsen. In fact it has been in her wardrobe as long as THAT favourite Collette Dinnigan dress - she often wears them together for weddings or garden parties. The Duchess is not the only Royal to favour the Danish company, set up by Keld Mikkelsen and his former partner Malene Birger - Crown Princess Mary of Denmark, whom Kate has met on several occasions, named Malene Birger 'the country's best designer'. Perhaps she gave Kate fashion tips. Certainly she has been immortalised on postage stamps. Just like Kate.

Alice Temperley Odele Sheepskin Coat

Like many A-listers, Kate has a number of Alice Temperley's whimsical frocks in her wardrobe - who can forget the black and nude Amoret gown she wore to the premiere of War Horse? But it is Temperley's £2,350 Odele coat which she chooses to wrap up in when the weather is cold. Kate wears the sheepskin, with its fur lining and leather trim, when she is out and about in town. Temperley has always been a favourite with celebrities such as Scarlett Johansson, Emma Watson and Keira Knightley - her designs are sold around the world - but it was Kate's sister Pippa who put Alice Temperley on the Royal map when she wore an emerald gown to the evening do after the Royal Wedding.

Favourite Jackets

'We design with a woman like Kate Middleton in mind: tailored and effortlessly chic – Andrea Lenczner and Christie Smythe

Smythe Les Vestes Blazer

Kate loves her £575 Duchess blazer so much that she has it in two - traditional military - colours: navy blue and army green. She wore the blue one on her first tour of Canada (she has since worn it more than any other jacket) and the green one on her second tour, showing the diplomacy which has become her trademark. The jacket, designed by Canadians Andrea Lenczner and Christie Smythe, sold out on Net-A-Porter.com within 15 minutes of her arrival at the airport. Apparently the pair had known for weeks that she was considering wearing it. But it was only when she donned it, on the morning of her departure for Canada, that they were certain. Kate is not the only celebrity fan of the company, which was set up in 2004 - Heidi Klum and Rachel McAdams also wear their beautifully-tailored designs.

LK Bennett Darwin Sheepskin Jacket

When winter comes, there is only one jacket in the Duchess of Cambridge's wardrobe - LK Bennett's Darwin sheepskin jacket. Kate is a huge fan of the High Street label and is regularly spotted wearing this £695 shearling, with its nipped in waist. Its first outing was when the newly-wed went to watch her husband play football on Christmas Eve in the village of Castle Rising - before her first Royal Christmas at Sandringham.

Favourite Dresses

'It is a delight to dress her—
she has such a great sense of
style, and she dresses
very appropriately.'
– Collette Dinnigan

Collette Dinnigan Champagne Lace Cocktail Dress

This stunning Moonstone cap sleeve cocktail dress in musk metallic lace is by one of Australia's most successful fashion designers and has been in Kate's wardrobe since way before her marriage. Dating from summer 2006, it is one of her go-to dresses for Royal – or society - weddings. She first wore it for the nuptials of William's stepsister Laura Parker Bowles and old Etonian former Calvin Klein model Harry Lopes. You also might have spotted a glimpse of it at the marriage ceremony of William's cousin Zara Phillips and former England Rugby caption Mike Tindall. Kate shows exquisite taste in her choice of designer: Collette, who was the first Australian to show during Paris Fashion Week, is a favourite with celebrities.

Stella McCartney Ridley Stretch Dress

There was only one fashion designer on everyone's lips during the 2012 London Olympics - Stella McCartney. The daughter of Beatle Sir Paul, who studied fashion design at London's Central Saint Martins College, designed the official Olympic Games wardrobe. So it was only fitting that Kate wore her Ridley Stretch Cady Dress for the Olympics Exhibition at London's National Portrait Gallery and to watch Andy Murray win his quarter final tennis match at Wimbledon. Afterwards McCartney was named Designer of the Year and was awarded an OBE. However the dress was not relegated to second division. Kate pulled it out of her wardrobe two years later for a SportsAid reception and two years after that for the Royal International Air Tattoo.

Runners Up

Amanda Wakeley Sculpted Felt Seam dress
Kate has this £450 figure-hugging sheath dress in creamy oatmeal and gunmetal grey.

Emilia Wickstead Alice dress
The Duchess has worn the £1,300 dress in pink and teal.

French Connection Cezanne Dress
We have seen Kate wear the green Great Plains and winter pink Paintbow dress. Both cost £48.

Favourite T-shirt

'I reckon we could have sold ten times as many.' – Clare Hornby.

ME + EM Cobalt Stripe Breton Top

This £48 t-shirt sparked a furore when Kate wore it at the Beaufort Polo Club six weeks after giving birth to Princess Charlotte. Within hours it had appeared on 40 news and fashion websites, sold out in all five colourways and had a 5,000-strong waiting list. So, what is the secret of Kate's miracle slimming top? Apparently, the key is the fabric - it is half- cotton and half-Lyocell, which means that the t-shirt retains its shape and covers lumps and bumps. It is also subtly ruched to cover up any post-pregnancy bulge. Kate loves this t-shirt so much that she has it in three colourways: white with blue stripes, cobalt blue with white stripes and white with black stripes. She discovered it after ME + EM founder Clare Hornby, sister-in-law of Fever Pitch author Nick, sent her staff a copy of her monthly magazine.

Favourite Jeans

'The skinny pant is here to stay. No matter what else is happening on the catwalks, it's a bestseller, year in year out.'
– Jeff Rudes.

J Brand 811

When the Duchess of Cambridge goes casual, she turns to her favourite J Brand navy jeans. The 811 Mid Rise Skinny leg jeans - which are 98 per cent cotton and two per cent lycra - are a staple in her wardrobe. They are made of stern stuff - she has worn them to the cinema, playing volleyball and dragon boat racing.

The cult jeans company, which was launched in Los Angeles in 2004 by former Abercrombie & Fitch man Jeff Rudes, is a winner with celebrities and fashionistas. The company has collaborated with two of Kate's favourite designers: Christopher Kane and Erdem. So they have to be a hit.

Favourite Shoes and Boots

'The princess purchased her Aquatalia boots directly, so she is a true brand fan.'
- Aquatalia.

Aquatalia Hi and Dry Boots

What does one wear for one's first festive season at Sandringham? A pair of Aquatalia boots, naturally. Kate donned the black suede classics on Christmas Day for the largest gathering of the Royals in years. Sadly the Duke of Edinburgh missed the outing as he was in hospital recovering from heart surgery. Kate made an inspired choice of designer - Aquatalia founder Marvin Krasnow, who trained in engineering before working in his family's shoe factory, is credited with creating the first weatherproof boots. Just what one needs for that Sandringham snow.

LK Bennett Sledge Shoes

She may not have worn them since 2014, but these £195 nude heels have become Kate's signature shoe. She has worn the patent pumps more than anything else. They are so ubiquitous that they have even been displayed in the Victoria & Albert Museum. However the Sledge risks being knocked off its pedestal by a younger, more elegant rival – the Fern, with its pointed toe and lower heel. Perfect for those Royal walkabouts.

Stuart Weitzman Cocoswoon Wedges

These £245 navy blue suede wedges have given the Sledge a run for its money. Despite their vertiginous height - the wedge is four and a half inches while the platform is one and a half inches - Kate has worn them on numerous occasions. Who can forget her first solo public appearance after the birth of Prince George, when she took part in an impromptu volleyball session at the Queen Elizabeth Olympic Park?

The ultimate warm weather essential: wear with anything from denim to pretty dresses for chic, understated style - fit for a princess.
Stuart Weitzman

Favourite Hats

Sylvia Fletcher for Lock & Co Black Fairytale Headpiece and Brown Betty Boop Hat

When Kate needs a hat, she often turns to milliner Lock & Co, which is a favourite with the Royals. The red Maple Leaf hat, which she wore for the Canada Day celebrations on her first Royal tour, was designed by Sylvia Fletcher - as were her favourite two hats - her £285 black Fairy Tale headpiece and her £245 brown Betty Boop hat. She first wore the Fairy Tale, which has a large felt flower on its brim, on her Diamond Jubilee visit to Leicester with The Queen and Duke of Edinburgh, while she wore the Betty Boop, with a bow on its brim, for her first solo military engagement to present shamrocks to the Irish Guards at Aldershot. Lock & Co, founded in 1676 to wait upon the court at St James', made the first bowler hat and supplied Admiral Lord Nelson. It has the Royal Warrant from the Prince of Wales. How better to please your father-in-law?

'Kate has got it all. She's beautiful and has a very good sense of style.'
Sylvia Fletcher.

Favourite Bag

Mulberry Bayswater Clutch

Kate loves her £495 Bayswater so much that she has it in three colours - black, burgundy and beige. But it is the black suede envelope clutch that is the firm winner. It has accompanied Kate on Royal tours of Australia and New Zealand, New York and Los Angeles; been spotted at film premieres and weddings; attended Trooping the Colour and the Remembrance Day service; and even met the cast of Downton Abbey. In fact it is almost as well travelled as she is.

Favourite Gloves

Cornelia James Imogen Merino Wool Glove with Side Bow

If you are a member of the Royal family there is - was - only one glove designer: the woman that Vogue magazine dubbed 'the colour Queen of England'. Official glove maker to The Queen - she was granted the Royal Warrant in 1979 - Cornelia James began making gloves for the Royals when designer Norman Hartnell asked James to create a pair for the young Princess Elizabeth's going away outfit. Since then her company has designed gloves for almost every member of the Royal family: the Queen Mother had elbow-length satin gloves to match her gowns; Princess Diana wore gloves to cover her bitten nails; Princess Beatrice donned them for the Royal Wedding and the Duchess of Cambridge wore long silk gloves for a diplomatic ball. But it is the £70 Imogen gloves which are her favourite - she has three pairs - in black, chocolate brown and navy.

'The Imogen glove encapsulates everything that is Cornelia James, classic, stylish and making an occasion of your everyday moments.' - Genevieve James.

Favourite Scarf

DC Dalgliesh Strathearn Tartan Scarf

When Kate is north of the border, she bears the title The Countess of Strathearn. So what better to wear than a hand-woven, hand-knotted silk scarf in the tartan favoured by the original Duke of Strathearn - son of Queen Victoria and great-great-great-great-great grandfather of Prince William?

The Duchess was given the £290 scarf by a guest at the Royal Wedding and first wore it at the Queen's Diamond Jubilee River Pageant. Since then it has become a favourite in Scotland.

According to legend Prince Edward, Duke of Strathearn, who was Colonel of the Royal Scots Regiment, sent a sample to Wilsons of Bannockburn with a view to 'dressing the gallant corps'. It then became the adopted tartan of the Comrie Pipe Band.

'It's immensely pleasing that she didn't just wear it once like some celebrities but that it's become a bit of a wardrobe favourite.' - Nick Fiddes

Favourite Jewels

'I designed pearl earrings to work for any occasion and I am thrilled to see the Duchess wear my pearls so often.'
— Annoushka Ducas

Annoushka Classic Baroque Pearl Earring Drops

Diamonds may be a girl's best friend but Kate prefers pearls. She has worn these creamy white freshwater pearl earrings more often than any other piece of jewellery – apart from her wedding and engagement rings. However that does not mean the Duchess shuns diamonds. She either suspends them on Annoushka's £795 Eclipse Yellow Gold and Diamond Porcupine Hoop Earrings or Kiki McDonough's £500 Yellow Gold and Diamond Hoops. How nice to have the choice. The Duchess of Cambridge has long been a fan of Annoushka Ducas, who began designing cufflinks in 1990 at the age of 23 - her Russian mother, who sold seafood, wanted an unusual gift to give her favourite clients. Links of London was born three years later.

How to Dress for the Season

Black Tie

If William and Kate are invited to a Black Tie function, you can put money on the fact that the Duchess will wear a long dress. However, it is perfectly acceptable - some might say de rigeur nowadays - to show off your legs in a cocktail dress. If in doubt, copy Kate and wear BOTH. Remember the Jenny Packham pale blue gown she wore to the Natural History Museum's Photography Awards gala?

* *Accessorise with ....satin court shoes, diamond drop earrings and a statement bracelet.*

White Tie

If there is one rule for White Tie it is long, long, long. Whether you want to champion Ice Queen Grace Kelly, sex siren Sophia Loren, blonde bombshell Marilyn Monroe or elfin actress Audrey Hepburn, invest in a floor-length gown AND breathe a sigh that you can, for once, hide your pins. But, whatever you do, don't mistake dressing up for exposing your assets. No matter how tempting, never wear a dress slashed to the thigh or plunging to the navel. If in doubt, copy Kate. Her favourite evening wear designers are Alice Temperley, Amanda Wakeley and Jenny Packham. No wonder. They make her look like a princess.

* *Accessorise with ....strappy sandals, long gloves and a tiara.*

White Tie

Ascot

Lounge Suits

When your invitation reads lounge suits, that does not mean you will be lounging around. Instead it signifies PARTY. So do not wear a dressing gown and pyjamas but release your inner siren and dress for FUN. Avoid anything which symbolises work - suits, leather and ballet pumps. Instead go mad with lace, velvet, jewels and feathers.

✳ Accessorise with ... funky jewellery, vintage bags and skyscraper heels. Always carry ballet pumps in your bag.

Ascot

There is nothing better than a pretty floral or lace dress for a day at the races. Who can forget Kate in her summery white lace Dolce & Gabbana number? But it is the hat that will give you the wow factor. Wear a statement hat for Ladies' Day - it is the one occasion in the social calendar when you can go to town. Just remember not to block the view of the race. Afterall, that's what the day is supposed to be about.

✳ Accessorise with ... wedges or block heels, short gloves and a knockout hat.

Weddings

Whatever you do, DON'T wear white, DON'T expose your boobs and DON'T upstage the bride. However DO abandon fears about wearing black. It is perfectly acceptable nowadays. Just remember the Duchess of Cambridge in THAT velvet Libélula coat. The world lusted after it. Equally red is - contrary to popular belief - positively perfect. Think Kate in Issa or Collette Dinnigan.

* Accessorise with ....discreet jewellery, low sling-backs or court shoes and a headpiece NOT a fascinator.

Garden Parties

It's not obligatory to wear a hat at a Buckingham Palace garden party but it is etiquette. Kate usually wears a coat dress - her favourites are Alexander McQueen and Emilia Wickstead - with a matching hat. Not to mention her favourite nude heels.

* Accessorise with .... pearl earrings, clutch bag and wide smile.

Garden Parties

The Essentials...

British fashionistas have always been known for their quirky style. But society girls know that the key to dressing for the season is to invest in classics and shop for trends on the High Street. How else would one cope with one's whirlwind social life?

...Coats

The Barbour

No self-respecting Sloane would be without her favourite Barbour jacket and Kate is no exception - she has at least four in her wardrobe which she wears for walking her dog Lupo.

The Sheepskin

Kate owns two sheepskins - one for the country, one for town. She wears her black Alice Temperley Odele coat when she is shopping in the capital, while she brings out her brown LK Bennett Darwin jacket in the countryside.

The Blazer

Everygirl worth her salt has got a navy blazer, which she wears with jeans or a summer dress. The Duchess of Cambridge has two - a single-breasted version from Smythe Les Vestes and a double-breasted one from Zara.

The Winter Coat

Kate has a number of coats in her closet, which she
tends to wear with a belt. She favours two silhouettes -
a nipped-in waist and full skirt reminiscent of Christian
Dior's New Look - and a fitted straight coat, also
popular in the 1950s. However she does not distinguish
between High End and High Street designers and has
both. Favourites include Catherine Walker, Christopher
Kane, Goat, Hobbs, Jonathan Saunders, Matthew
Williamson, Missoni, Mulberry and Reiss.

The Tweed

Being a country girl, Kate has always known the
importance of having tweed in your wardrobe for events
such as the Cheltenham Races. Her favourite go-to
designers are Katherine Hooker and Moloh.

The Cocktail Coat

Sometimes a wool or cashmere coat doesn't cut it: one
needs a velvet, silk or brocade coat for weddings, parties
and special occasions. Kate is fortunate enough to have
a choice between a black velvet Libélula coat and two
brocade numbers by Jane Troughton and Day by
Malene Birger.

...Dresses

The Long Gown

It is hard not to be envious of Kate's array of glittering evening dresses - whether they are made from hand-spun lace, covered in sequins or decorated in crystals, she always sparkles. Top marks for Alice Temperley, Amanda Wakeley and Jenny Packham.

The Cocktail Dress

For most girls, a cocktail dress is a wardrobe staple - although Kate prefers long dresses to short. However even she cannot resist a little black dress. Actually she has several little black lace dresses - by Dolce & Gabbana, Beulah, Jenny Packham and Temperley. She also has white lace cocktail dresses by Collette Dinnigan and Lela Rose.

The Wrap Dress

There cannot be many women who don't have a dress designed by Wrap Queen Diane von Furstenberg. Kate has owned a DVF paisley wrap since her student days - she wore it to a party at St Andrews University in 2002 and on a date with the student prince three years later.

The Tea Dress

Another wardrobe staple is the tea dress. Kate's favourite is a £475 Budding Hearts silk crepe de chine dress by retro designer Suzannah. You might remember it from the photographs marking Prince George's first birthday, which were taken at the Natural History Museum's Sensational Butterflies Exhibition.

The Fifties Classics

Kate loves dresses that evoke the 1950s, a decade renowned for its elegance. She has endless shift dresses in her wardrobe as well as wasp-waisted gowns with full skirts. If you want to follow in her footsteps, shop at Alexander McQueen, Catherine Walker, Emilia Wickstead, Erdem, Roksanda Ilinic and Stella McCartney. Alternatively copy her look at French Connection, Hobbs, Joseph, LK Bennett, Reiss and Whistles.

...Shoes and Boots

The Court Shoes

As every girl knows, you can never have too many pairs of shoes in your wardrobe - especially court shoes. Invest in classic colours - black, navy, chocolate, charcoal and nude in suede, patent and satin - and you can't go far wrong.

The Ballet Pumps

High heels are very well but sometimes a girl needs a pair of ballet pumps to rest one's weary feet. The Duchess of Cambridge buys hers from French Sole. She is a regular in their King's Road and Knightsbridge shops and favours their India pumps.

The Wedges

If you want to walk tall during the summer, you should invest in a pair of wedges - they are perfect for a day at the races. Kate owns several pairs in classic colours - navy, black and cream - although there are rumours that The Queen does not approve. She has even been known to jump hurdles and play hockey in them.

The Plimsolls

A pair of plimsolls is pretty much a wardrobe essential - just ask the French. Kate's come from Mint Velvet - she owns the £89 Bibi grey suede ones.

The Winter Boots

You can't survive a British winter without owning several pairs of boots: the aristocracy favours long brown leather riding boots - flats and heels - for the countryside and black suede ones - heels - for town. Throw in a pair of ankle boots and you're set for every occasion.

The Wellington Boots

You can't live in the British countryside without owning a pair of wellies. Named after the 1st Duke of Wellington, they became a staple of the hunting, shooting and fishing brigade in the 19th century. The Royals buy theirs from Le Chameau - Kate owns the £170 Vierzon Nord boots, which ironically are crafted in France.

The Walking Boots

Equally a pair of walking boots is essential for enjoying the elements. Kate's Brasher Hillmaster GTX boots are made by British firm Berghaus and cost £160. They first saw action in the Borneo rainforest.

The Deck Shoes

If you have the sailing bug, you need a pair of deck shoes, preferably made by American firm Sebago. You can't go wrong with Kate's favourite Bala Boat Shoes - her £94.99 moccasins come in taupe suede and white leather and are hand sewn.

... Accessories

The Tod Bag

If you are a Royal fan there is one bag you HAVE to get your hands on - Tod's £1013 D-Styling Bauletto Medio - although it won't be easy as it has been discontinued. Named after the late Princess Diana, Kate has a modernised version in grey - she was snapped carrying it leaving a Christmas carol concert just after her engagement.

The Clutch Bag

Vintage or modern, velvet or suede, a classic clutch is the most useful bag in one's wardrobe. Kate buys some on the High Street (Hobbs, LK Bennett, Russell & Bromley), has designer ones (Anya Hindmarch, Emmy, Mulberry and Prada) and even has them made to match her dresses (Alexander McQueen and Jenny Packham).

Gloves

There is only one place to buy one's gloves if you want to copy the Royal family - Royal Warrant holder Cornelia James. She has a selection of long silk evening gloves in ivory and black as well as wool gloves in black, navy and chocolate.

Hats

One can never have enough hats if one is a social butterfly. After all, one needs a knockout hat for Ascot - not to mention a selection of summer straws, glittering cocktail headpieces and winter velours to see you through the season. For inspiration check out Prince George's christening - Kate looked fabulous in Jane Taylor, Pippa sensational in this Edwina Ibbotson headpiece, Camilla wore Philip Treacy and Carole Middleton donned Jane Corbett. Her Majesty's hat was made by her dresser Angela Kelly.

Q&A Daniella Helayel

She may come from Rio but Daniella KNOWS how to dress a princess. It was she who designed the Issa Forever gown that Kate wore on the day of her engagement. She now has her own label Dhela.

Q: How would you define British style?

A: It is a mix of classic and eccentric with a twist.

Q: What do you think the essential dresses are in a British woman's wardrobe?

A: Long-sleeved dresses and belted dresses are very flattering and very versatile. They can take you to cocktails and dinner and will suit anybody.

Q: When should one wear black?

A: When you are feeling bloated or for a funeral - or, to be honest, any time you want and feel right. There are no dos and don'ts.

Q: What should you wear for Black Tie?

A: I personally prefer long for Black Tie. But a short sparkly number could be good too.

Q: What should you wear on the red carpet?

A: A stunning gown would be my choice - something that leaves a trace behind and is quite dramatic.

Q: Are there any fashion rules?

A: My rule is always feel good and anything will work - as long as you are comfortable in your own skin.

Q: How would you dress for a dinner party?

A: Dresses! Dresses and dresses! A good dress will take you anywhere.

Q: What about wedding guests?

A: I would not wear white for a wedding - that is the bride's colour. You can wear black but it is much nicer to wear a bejewelled colour like Royal blue, emerald green or ruby red. Colours make people look so much more beautiful. They lighten up your complexion.

Q: What about colour?

A: Most British ladies stick to a traditional palette of black, ivory and nude. This is such a shame as there are some amazing colours, which can be more flattering and just as practical. Did you know that red is in fact invisible under white?

Q: Do you have views on tights versus bare legs?

A: Not really. I wear tights in the winter as I'm always cold but in the summer I always prefer bare legs.

Q: When should you wear tights, stockings and bare legs?

A: This really is a matter of personal preference - the weather and, of course, how good your legs are!

Q&A June Kenton

June Kenton, who owns Royal Warrant Holder Rigby & Peller is THE Queen of Lingerie. She has been providing bespoke underwear for The Monarch since 1960 and is a favourite with the Royal family.

Q: How would you define British Style?

A: British style is elegant, refined and feminine.

Q: Do you need different lingerie for different outfits?

A: Absolutely. You cannot underestimate the importance of shape here - in addition to fit of course.

Q: What do you think are the essential items of lingerie in a woman's wardrobe?

A: An everyday bra which makes you feel fabulous - it should fit like a glove and be styled to perfection (whether a full cup, balcony, plunge or soft cup, this is likely to become your go-to shape); a t-shirt bra; a statement piece; a sports bra; a strapless bra; solution wear.

Q: What are your thoughts on matching bras and knickers?

A: Absolutely! I've campaigned all my life to tell everyone to wear matching bra and knickers. It can provide a real confidence boost.

Q: Should you ever reveal your lingerie?

A: Only reveal your lingerie if it fits and suits you perfectly. I think it's acceptable to see a hint of a strap - if it's pretty.

Marie Jo...

Q&A Jane Winkworth

Jane Winkworth is the woman who turned the humble ballet pump into a fashion classic. She set up French Sole in 1989 and counts the Duchess amongst her customers.

Q: What colour shoes are essential for the British style icon?
A: Black patent.

Q: How would you define British style?
A: Safe and classical. It's not overly colourful, or flamboyant and it's certainly not 'stand out from the crowd'. It is discreet and reflects quality.

Q: How many pairs of shoes or boots does a girl need?
A: Unlimited if possible! Shoes should be replaced each season - with the exception of high quality evening shoes. Six pairs of shoes, three pairs of boots each season, excluding occasion shoes, should suffice.

Q: What shoes should one wear with an evening dress?
A: With a long evening dress, one can get away with a mid-heel strappy sandal, with a touch of glitter. I love gold and silver metallic heels for parties! For a short dress, I think one should wear a low to mid-heel, traditional pointed court shoe. These for me should be delicate, very pretty and of course, sparkly.

Q: What shoes should one wear to a wedding?
A: Definitely heels, but low slingbacks or court shoes. You never want to draw too much attention to yourself or take away from the bride.

Q: What shoes should one wear to Ascot? To the Races?
A: Wedges or low block heels are perfect for a day at the races and, of course, ballet flats in your bag!

Q: What shoes should one wear to a nightclub?
A: For me it's the one time you can wear a pair of Manolos and allow crazy, exotic and flamboyant colours and textures.

Q: What is your view on matching shoes and bags?
A: Horrendous! In my world, this is pretty much a no go - except a small clutch that matches your shoes.

Q&A Rachel Trevor-Morgan

Royal Warrant holder Rachel Trevor-Morgan has been The Queen's milliner since 2006 - she designs many of Her Majesty's hats to co-ordinate with dress sketches at her 17th century studio in London's St James's.

Q: How would you define British style?

A: Stylish and chic - with a twist of eccentricity.

Q: How many hats should a girl own?

A: At least one but preferably more. Too many women don't have any these days which is a tragedy! Everyone should have one black hat for hat 'emergencies' - they work with any outfit. Otherwise find your own signature style. Don't be afraid to step outside your comfort zone.

Q: When should you wear a hat?

A: It is best to check your invite as it is sometimes stipulated that hats are compulsory (or not!).

Q: When would you wear a hat?

A: I would wear a hat at every given opportunity. I sometimes wear a headdress to dinner parties and champagne receptions - they are fun and a great talking point. And, in the winter months, I often wear one of my classic felt trilbies - or a cap - as they are practical and warm.

Q: Which hats should you wear in the summer and which hats in the winter?

A: Rules nowadays are a lot more relaxed than in previous decades. There was a time when you would never be seen in a straw in winter or a felt in summer. If in doubt, a small silk hat is the perfect cross-season choice.

Q: Are there any events where it is obligatory to wear a hat?

A: If you are in the Royal Enclosure at Royal Ascot, then you have to adhere to strict rules. Your hat or headpiece must have a base of at least ten centimetres. You must wear a hat in the presence of HM The Queen when attending a Royal garden party or an investiture.

Q: How do you greet someone if you are wearing a hat?

A: I always think it is more important to look good and feel confident rather than worry about kissing your guests!

Q: What type of hat would you wear for Ascot? The races? A wedding? Church?

A: For Royal Ascot I would always advise going for a bold statement hat - after all, dressing up for Royal Ascot is all about millinery. If you are going to Cheltenham, hat wearing is more casual and 'country' – think felt trilbies and fedoras. For a wedding, consider whether the wedding is in the country or in town. Wear a hat but consider the bride and her mother - you wouldn't want to outshine them. It saddens me that people don't wear hats to church any more. My mother was known for her Sunday hats - I am sure that's where my love of millinery comes from. Wear what you feel comfortable in; if you want to dress up then do!

Q&A Genevieve Lawson

Cornelia James, which was set up by Genevieve's mother, has been The Queen's official glove maker since 1947 - couturier Norman Hartnell asked her to make the then Princess Elizabeth's going-away gloves for her wedding to Lt Philip Mountbatten. The firm was granted a Royal Warrant in 1979.

Q: How would you define British style?

A: Iconic, avant-garde and timeless.

Q: Are gloves fashionable?

A: Gloves are more a question of style rather than fashion.

Q: When should one wear gloves?

A: Formal occasions of course - but wearing gloves just adds that touch of class.

Q: How many pairs of gloves should a girl own?

A: A girl should own a wardrobe of gloves, for every event and for every occasion. An outfit without gloves is like a sentence without punctuation!

Q: When would you wear them?

A: I wear them often - merino wool gloves for business meetings; evening gloves for Glyndebourne; leather gloves for driving; cashmere gloves for dog walking and ski gloves for the slopes.

Q: When should one wear long gloves?

A: Long gloves for formal occasions, such as attending the State Opening of Parliament or banquets at Buckingham Palace or the Guildhall.

Q: When should one wear short gloves?

A: Short gloves for a daytime wedding, visit to Royal Ascot - or when you want to add that finishing touch to your outfit.

Q: How do you eat with gloves?

A: We design a pure silk glove called Desdemona, which has a button opening on the inside of the wrist called a mousquetaire. You unbutton the mousquetaire and roll the hand part of the glove under the opening. So you still retain the effect of wearing gloves but the hands remain uncovered.

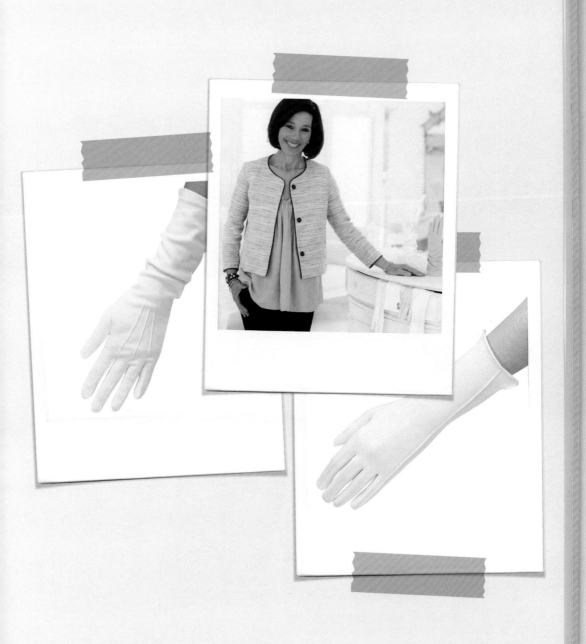

Q&A Harry Collins

Harry Collins, owner of family firm G Collins & Sons, has the honour of being Her Majesty's personal jeweller. He has his own workshop at Buckingham Palace, where he cleans and repairs The Queen's magnificent jewellery collection.

Q: How would you define British style?

A: Pearls, pearls, pearls. They are classic, understated and refined; can be worn with any colour and are tasteful and elegant. Essential in every lady's jewellery box.

Q: What do you think are the essential pieces of jewellery for a British lady?

A: One must have a single classic row of pearls, which can be graduated, knotted onto a classic clasp. Perhaps a double or triple-string pearl necklace too. Complement them with a pair of single stud earrings for daytime and a pair of drop pearls for evening wear - pear-shaped natural pearls are beautiful but very expensive. A pearl brooch is always useful - maybe an antique circle, which never dates. Diamond earrings are also important - when one talks to people one looks at their eyes but, when a lady is wearing diamond studs, one is constantly drawn to the earrings. A complementary diamond single stone pendant is nice - again nothing too fussy. Keep it simple.

Q: How should you keep your pearls?

A: They should always be protected in a natural silk purse or cover. The average jewellery box has a lot of acids in the material that will damage pearls.

Q: Should one wear matching earrings, necklace and bracelet?

A: Personally, I prefer jewellery pieces to complement each other, rather than match exactly.

Q: When should one wear pearls and when should one wear diamonds?

A: Pearls are an ideal item of jewellery to wear when going to meet the possible future in-laws. They are classic and unpretentious. On the wrist you could wear a Patek Philippe watch and a small claw-set platinum diamond-line bracelet. For a formal evening event, such as a ball, a diamond-line necklace is perfect. You could get your jeweller to create a clever fitting so you can hang pearls from your existing diamond studs and pendant. It looks stunning at a fraction of the cost. If you really want to wow at an event, wear a stunning pair of drop earrings and a very wide diamond bracelet - perhaps Art Deco.

Q: What should one wear on a date?

A: When on a date, avoid rings on any fingers that could look like an old engagement ring - and do not wear any heart shapes that could be a gift from an ex. Maybe wear a nice pair of earrings and pendant - so that he knows he has to keep you in the manner you are accustomed to!

Q: What should one wear to Ascot?

A: The sky is the limit but don't wear a tiara - these are reserved for weddings or special Royal occasions.

Q: What jewellery should one wear to a wedding and a christening?

A: For weddings, one simple rule of jewellery, never outdo the bride. Christenings, stay understated.

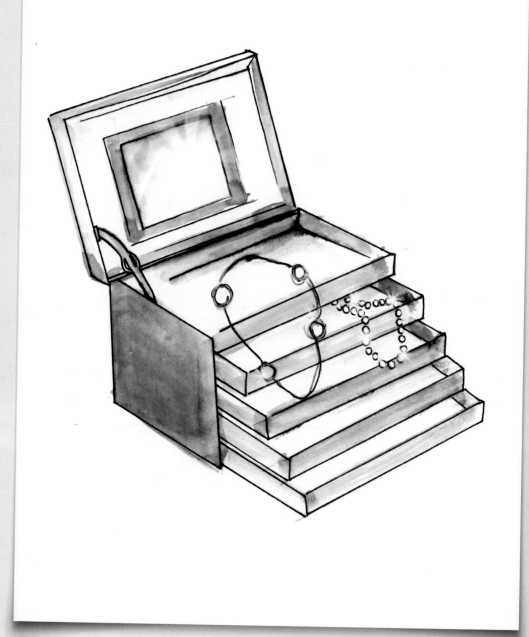

The Crown Jewels: Kate's £600,000 Jewellery Collection

Necklaces £164,000+

TIFFANY
£800

G COLLINS & SONS
£8,475

MOUAWAD
£75,000+

MONICA VINADER
£1,950

TOP LEFT TO RIGHT: KIKI MCDONOUGH £1,400 • ASPREY £3,300 • MAPPIN & WEBB £3,950 • MAPPIN & WEBB £2,000
MIDDLE LEFT TO RIGHT: LOLA ROSE £45 • KRISTIN MAGNUSSON £189 • CARTIER £55,500
BOTTOM LEFT TO RIGHT: MERCI MAMAN £79 • ASPREY £3,200 • ASPREY £4,300 • ASPREY £4,600

Earrings

£123,000+

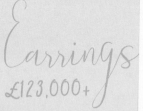

MONICA VINADER
£745

CARTIER
£35,700

CASSANDRA GOAD
£1,685

PIPPA SMALL
£850

VINNIE DAY
£126

KIKI MCDONOUGH
£2,500

KIKI MCDONOUGH
£1,400

BEAUT'S VINTAGE
£195

CZ BY KENNETH LANE
£130

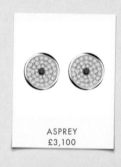

ASPREY
£3,100

LINKS OF LONDON
£140

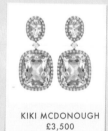

KIKI MCDONOUGH
£3,500

KIKI MCDONOUGH
£2,400

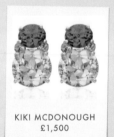

KIKI MCDONOUGH
£1,500

MONICA VINADER
£125

KIKI MCDONOUGH
£4,500

KIKI MCDONOUGH
£3,400

KIKI MCDONOUGH
£7,500

BALENCIAGA
£415

CATHERINE ZORAIDA
£150

CATHERINE ZORAIDA
£150

KIKI MCDONOUGH
£2,200

MIRABELLE
£35

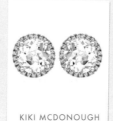

KIKI MCDONOUGH
£495

KIKI MCDONOUGH
£795

ROBINSON PELHAM
£15,000

MAPPIN & WEBB
£3,750

LINKS OF LONDON
£325

PATRICK MAVROS
£170

TIFFANY
£595

ROBINSON PELHAM
£14,300

KIKI MCDONOUGH
£2,600

KIKI MCDONOUGH
£1,400

G COLLINS & SONS
£8,750

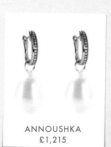

AMRAPALI
£1,362

ANNOUSHKA
£1,215

OSCAR DE LA RENTA
£178

OSCAR DE LA RENTA
£168

SORU JEWELLERY
£130

Rings £301,000+

* Not the actual rings

GARRARD
£300,00+

WARTSKI
£500+

ANNOUSHKA
£995

Watches £5,000+

TISSOT
£620

CARTIER
£4,600

Bracelets £19,000+

TIFFANY
£730

TIFFANY
£480

MOUAWAD
£18,000+

CATHERINE ZORAIDA
£430

By Royal Appointment: An A-Z of Kate's Designers

A is for... Alexander McQueen

No A-Z of the Duchess of Cambridge's wardrobe would be complete without the name Alexander McQueen. After all the label's designer Sarah Burton created the world's most-talked-about (and most secretive) wedding gown. She kept the public and the fashion world guessing for months - and even kept her parents in the dark - about landing the plum commission. Since then she has been named Designer of the Year, received an OBE and become Kate's go-to designer. Not bad for the woman who joined McQueen straight out of Central St Martins College in 1997 – the first question Lee (as McQueen was known) asked her was: 'Do you believe in UFO's?' Sadly McQueen, who was her boss, friend and mentor, committed suicide in 2010 and Burton reluctantly took over the helm.

'We put our hearts into it...It was a magical experience' - Sarah Burton.

B is for...Beulah

'I think she just really likes the collection and the ethical values behind it.'
— Lady Natasha Rufus Isaacs.

Beulah London is the ethical luxury fashion label run by Prince William's childhood friend Lady Natasha Rufus Isaacs (who in a twist of fate is married to Kate's former boyfriend, solicitor Rupert Finch) and her friend Lavinia Brennan, who moves in equally-elevated circles (she once dated the actor Jack Fox, son of James, nephew of Edward and brother of Laurence). 'Nats' and 'Lavs', as they are known to their friends, created the red Sarai evening gown Kate wore for her first 100 Women in Hedge Funds charity dinner – and Kate has a number of their creations in her wardrobe. Not to mention the fact that the two history of art graduates, who met in the congregation of Holy Trinity Brompton and travelled to India to do voluntary work, have designed some of Kate's favourite scarves.

C is for... Charlotte Todd

Who can forget THAT dress? Fashion and textiles student Charlotte Todd created the £30 diaphanous dress for her Bristol University brief 'the art of seduction' and seduce it definitely did. Kate waltzed down the catwalk at St Andrews University in the hand-knitted silk jersey tube and William, who had paid £200 for his ticket, turned to his friend Fergus Boyd and said: 'Wow Kate's hot.' Auctioneer Kerry Taylor called it the dress that 'caught a prince's eye and then his heart'. It sold for £78,000.

'It was designed as a skirt but I'm not sure it would have had such an impact on William if Kate had worn it as I intended.' - Charlotte Todd

D is for... Diane von Furstenberg

Not only has it paid for my children's education and my houses and my freedom, but it has had a huge influence on millions of women.
Diane von Furstenberg

This Queen of the wrap dress is one of Kate's favourite designers – when she wore a DVF Patrice dress in a navy Ikat Batik print on tour in Sydney in 2014 it sold out on the website in a record-breaking eight minutes. The iconic dress, coded T72, made its debut in a fashion show at Manhatten's Pierre Hotel in 1974. Since then it has made the designer millions and kept her on the Forbes list of The World's 100 Most Powerful Women and Time magazine's The 100 Most Influential People. She's almost as important as Kate.

E is for... Erdem

'I've got huge respect for women and I love the idea of creating something that makes someone feel beautiful and comfortable in their own skin.'
— Erdem Moralioglu.

When she stepped off the plane for her first Royal tour of Canada, the Duchess of Cambridge proved she was a true diplomat - she wore a stone crepe and navy lace Cecile shift dress by young Turk Erdem Moralioglu, who grew up in Montreal and is now a star of London's fashion scene. The son of a Turkish father and English mother designed his first dress at the age of seven for his twin sister's Barbie. He has come a long way since then - his dresses are worn by Royalty (Kate has a selection of his designs in her wardrobe including the green Allie coat she wore at the Tour de France), politicians of all spectrums (Michelle Obama, Sam Cam and Sarah Brown) and Hollywood celebrities (Kiera Knightley, Anne Hathaway, Jessica Alba). So it was no surprise he was named 2014 Designer of the Year.

F is for... French Sole

Every girl needs a pair of ballet pumps and Kate is no exception. The Duchess regularly drops in to French Sole in London's King's Road or Knightsbridge to buy her favourite Henrietta pumps. Designer Jane Winkworth, who was mad about ballet, was the woman who brought ballet pumps to Britain in 1989, launching as a mail-order company before opening her first shop in Fulham two years later. Princess Diana was a loyal customer. So is her daughter-in-law – as are Carole and Pippa Middleton, Princesses Beatrice and Eugenie.

'I am very lucky that the Middletons wear my shoes without me even asking.'
– Jane Winkworth

G is for... G Collins & Sons

This family firm in Tonbridge Wells has the accolade of being the Crown Jeweller. So when the Duchess of Cambridge found that her sapphire and diamond engagement ring was slipping off her finger, owner Harry Collins was the man she turned to. He fitted two small platinum beads – dubbed 'speed bumps' inside the ring, which belonged to Princess Diana, to make it a size I (her finger is a slim size H). Since then she has worn a G Collins & Sons necklace and earrings to the 2015 Service of Commemoration at St Paul's Cathedral to mark the end of combat operations in Afghanistan. But it was The Queen who was his first regal customer. She commissioned him to make a present for the Queen Mother's 100th birthday and was so delighted by the Centenary Rose brooch that she appointed him her Personal Jeweller, allowing him to set up a workshop within Buckingham Palace. His company – named after his father Gabriel – received a Royal Warrant in 2005. Two years later G Collins & Sons took over from Garrard as the Royals' favourite jeweller.

H is for...Hobbs

'She is a great supporter of UK fashion and she wears High Street right up to designer.' – Nicky Dulieu

No list of Kate's favourite shops would be complete without Hobbs, the High Street chain which has seen a turnaround since the arrival of Nicky Dulieu. Kate wore its Dalmatian print mackintosh on her last public engagement before giving birth to Prince George - it sold out within an hour. She is also a fan of its brown Celeste coat and its green Persephone coat. Hobbs was founded in 1981 by Yoram and Marilyn Anselm as a shoe shop, which was popular among Sloane Rangers, but it lost its way after expanding into fashion. Now it has the Royal seal of approval.

I is for... Issa

'It was a very special moment and we were very happy and grateful that she chose to wear one of my dresses on such a special occasion.' – Daniella Helayel

Who can forget the Royal blue Issa dress that the Duchess of Cambridge wore on the day she announced her engagement to Prince William? Kate picked up the off-the-peg gown from Fenwick, in London's Bond Street, paying the £385 price tag in full. She was already an aficionado of the label, which was launched by Brazilian Daniella Helayel in 2001, a year after arriving in London – the name echoes the surfer's 'cry of joy' when riding the perfect wave. Kate wore a number of Issa gowns before her engagement – she owns the iconic Lucky dress which was the summer hit of 2008 – but has stopped wearing them since Camilla al Fayed, the daughter of Harrods owner Mohammed Al-Fayed and sister of Dodi Fayed, took over the brand.

J is for... Jigsaw

There are not many companies which can boast of employing the Duchess of Cambridge. But Jigsaw owners Belle and John Robinson have that unique privilege. Kate worked at their head office in Kew as an accessories buyer before she married Prince William. She joined the company in 2006, working four days a week and left a year later (she was given an envelope of Jigsaw vouchers). Belle said afterwards: 'Kate supported a couple of Jigsaw events we did. Then she rang me up one day and said, "Could I come and talk to you about work?" She genuinely wanted a job but she needed an element of flexibility to continue the relationship with a very high-profile man and a life that she can't dictate.'

K is for... Kiki McDonough

My earrings take her from the school run through to formal evenings without a fuss. – Kiki McDonough

She is the Royals' favourite jeweller – and the Duchess of Cambridge is no exception. Kate owns more than a dozen sets of her colourful earrings, including a pair of Green Amethyst Yellow Gold and Diamond Oval Drops, which are believed to have been a Christmas present from Prince William in 2011, and the Green Tourmaline, Green Amethyst and Diamond earrings she was given as a present after the birth of Princess Charlotte. Kiki created her eponymous company in 1985 after she she fell in love with the Spring Fairy's pale blue and peridot tutu in a production of Sleeping Beauty. The Duchess of York wore a pair of McDonough diamond studs to announce her engagement to Prince Andrew and Princess Diana was a huge fan. Now the Duchess of Cambridge has taken over her mantle.

L is for...

It is safe to say that LK Bennett is one of Kate's favourite High Street stores. Her wardrobe must be cluttered with their dresses, coats and jackets – not to mention her ubiquitous nude Sledge heels and Natalie bag. Linda Kristin Bennett opened her first shop in Wimbledon in 1990 with £28,000 in loans and savings. Seventeen years later she sold her controlling stake to a private equity firm for roughly £70 million. All thanks to that nude court shoe.

Favourite shoes. ♡

M is for...Moloh

'We're delighted to see her supporting Moloh and flying the flag for British design'. - Caroline Smiley.

When the Countess of Strathearn – as she is known in Scotland - goes north of the border, she inevitably wears a flash of tartan. And who does she turn to? A country designer, who has a shop in the Gloucestershire town of Tetbury, a mile away from Highgrove, the private residence of her father-in-law Prince Charles and childhood home of her husband Prince William. She wore Moloh's Workers coat during a visit to Glasgow during the Commonwealth Games and chose a tweed Turpin coat for Christmas Day with the Middletons. Owner Caroline Smiley, who is a keen horsewoman, founded Moloh in 2003 and swiftly became a favourite of the country set.

N is for...Nike

Nearly every sports hero, rock star and Royal has a Nike label in their wardrobe and Kate is no exception. Whether she is sailing, playing hockey or tennis, she turns to the brand, which was founded in 1964 and takes its name from the Greek goddess of victory. So what did she pull out of her wardrobe when she attended one of tennis coach Judy Murray's Tennis on the Road workshops – this Pro Hyperwarm Half-Zip training top. Naturally.

O is for...Orla Kiely

'She is a wonderful person supporting many charities and important causes, a positive role model for our times.'
— Orla Kiely

You can barely walk into a middle-class British home without seeing an Orla Kiely mug, coaster or cushion. The Irish designer, who brought us laminated table cloths in brightly-coloured retro prints, has made the 1970s fashionable again. Kate is a fan of her Birdie print – she wore an Orla Kiely brown and cream shirt dress, which she bought half price in a sale for £162.50, for her third solo public engagement to the Art Room. She also has the label's grey pleated Daisy dress. Orla originally worked for a wallpaper designer before studying knitwear at the Royal College of Art. A decade after she launched her company, she had become so popular that she was featured on a postage stamp and awarded an OBE.

P is for... Peter Jones

When she got engaged, the Duchess of Cambridge was often spotted browsing at the Sloane Ranger's favourite department store. She nipped in to buy make-up – she was a frequent visitor to the Bobbi Brown counter, sitting on a stool on the shop floor for a free lesson (a beautician there is responsible for that 'Scouse brow') and has bought Prince William a Valentine's Day present in the men's department (Ralph Lauren boxer shorts, since you ask). Kate even popped in on the day of her first official evening engagement. Peter Jones is owned by the John Lewis Partnership, which opened its first store, a small drapers shop in Oxford Street, in 1864 (it took 16s 4d on the first day).

Q is for... The Queen

When The Queen made her acting debut alongside 007 in the Opening Ceremony of the London Olympics, she cemented her reputation as the People's Queen. But to the Duchess of Cambridge she is also grandmother-in-law. Since Kate married William she has been a gentle guiding influence, taking her under her wing, most memorably when they visited Fortnum & Mason with the Duchess of Cornwall during her Diamond Jubilee. And, when Kate has been stuck for a tiara or diamond brooch, it is to The Queen she has turned. Three cheers for Her Majesty.

'She's been a gentle guidance.' – The Duchess of Cambridge

R is for… Reiss

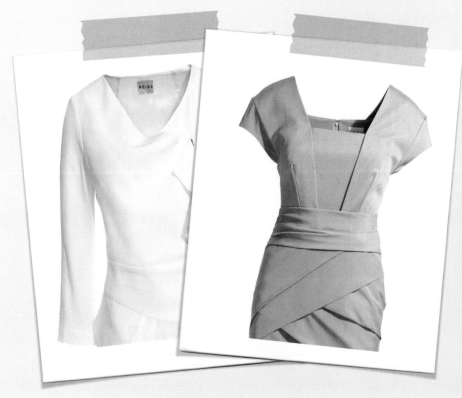

'Since Diana, there's been no one like her, and I'm very proud to be associated with her.' – David Reiss.

When Kate posed for her official engagement shoot with photographer Mario Testino she put High Street store Reiss firmly on the map. Its website immediately crashed and the cream Nanette frock sold out. Again when she wore the label's beige Shola shift to meet the Obamas, there was another spike in traffic. Not to mention her selection of Reiss coats. Great news for owner David Reiss, who founded the company in 1971. No wonder he is a fan.

S is for...Seraphine

'It is an immense honour that the Duchess chose a Seraphine dress for her official family photograph.'
- Cecile Reinaud

When the Duchess of Cambridge announced that she was pregnant for the first time, maternity label Seraphine launched an advertising campaign on London buses asking: 'Is it a girl? Is it a boy?' As we now know, it was a boy – Prince George. And, for his first official portrait, taken by her father Michael Middleton, what did Kate wear? Seraphine's Jolene dress. It was a coup for the fashion label, founded by French designer Cecile Reinaud in 2003. The dress sold out within two hours of the photograph's publication and led to a four-week mailing list. Since then sales have boomed thanks to the Kate Effect – the Duchess apparently has more than a dozen dresses by the designer in her wardrobe, including its powder blue Natasha coat, which is now sold with the tag line 'Worn by the Duchess of Cambridge'.

T is for...Topshop

Topshop was the first shop on the High Street to benefit from the Kate Effect. Just 24 hours after she wore their black and white minidress to work on her 25th birthday, it had sold out. Since then she has been spotted browsing the rails of its Kensington store and queueing for the till with other customers. She even chose one of Topshop's Boho numbers for her tour of India – although you are unlikely to spot her in the store anymore.

'Kate is not a fashion icon yet but she may become one so it is nice to see her wearing Topshop clothes.' – Topshop

U is for... United Kingdom

Since Kate joined The Firm, she has travelled around the world, promoting British fashion and flying the flag for the United Kingdom. She and Prince William were regulars at the Olympic Stadium during the 2012 London Olympics, toured Britain with The Queen during her Diamond Jubilee, have attended state banquets and hosted the Obamas at Kensington Palace. Together they have put Britain back on the map.

V is for... Vivien Sheriff

'She has quite a few of our pieces and luckily she wore one of ours today.'

Vivien Sheriff

All eyes were upon Kate when she made her first official public engagement on the Isle of Anglesey, where she and Prince William made their first home. So, in a nod to the local countryside, she chose a milliner inspired by Britain's 'natural beauty and abundant wildlife'. Vivien Sheriff, whose eponymous company is based in rural Wiltshire, designed the bespoke headpiece, which was made from silk velvet and adorned with vintage buttons and a cameo brooch, which Kate chose to launch the Atlantic 85 Lifeboat Hereford Endeavour.

W is for... Whistles

We are delighted that Catherine has chosen to wear Whistles in her engagement photographs. - Jane Shepherdson.

Another British label that reaped rewards after the Royal engagement was Whistles. Kate wore their ivory silk Amy blouse – renamed The Kate - for one of the official photos. Since then she has been one of their regular customers, wearing their Bella body con dress for the Diamond Jubilee concert AND the closing ceremony of the Olympic Games. Chief executive Jane Shepherdson transformed the label after she joined in 2008.

$\mathcal{X}$ is for... Xmas Jumper

You might have to give this snap of William and Kate in their Xmas jumpers a double take. After all it is not exactly as it seems. It is, in fact, a spoof image of the couple celebrating Christmas with the Middletons taken by

Bafta-winning photographer Alison Jackson. Using lookalikes, she created this festive scenario after Pippa revealed that their father Michael turned up one year in an inflatable sumo wrestler outfit.

Y is for...

'I invented the word 'glow' in this industry.' - Terry de Gunzburg.

There are not many make-up artists, models or fashionistas who don't have Touche Éclat in their handbags and the Duchess of Cambridge is no exception. The miracle click pen concealer, often described as 'eight hours of sleep in a tube', must have been a Godsend for Kate during those sleepless nights after the birth of Prince George and Princess Charlotte. Launched in 1992 by YSL Beauté's creative director, Terry de Gunzburg, dubbed the 'Steve Jobs of make-up', Touche Éclat is now one of the iconic products of all times – one sells every 10 seconds.

Z is for...

What is the perfect outfit for going on honeymoon? A cornflower blue dress by fashion chain Zara. The Spanish fashion giant was the label of choice for the Duchess and her sister the day after the Royal Wedding – Pippa travelled home in an aptly-coloured Royal blue blazer. They are in good company. Queen Letizia of Spain, Michelle Obama and Samantha Cameron are all customers of the label, which opened its first store in Spain in 1975 – the name Zara was derived from Zorba the Greek (Zorba clashed with the name of a local bar). There are now more than 6,000 Zara shops in 80 countries, including the UK.

Photo Credits

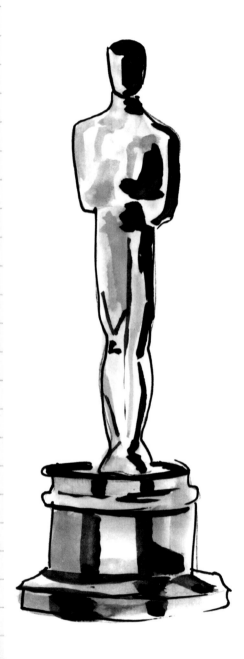

Photo Credits

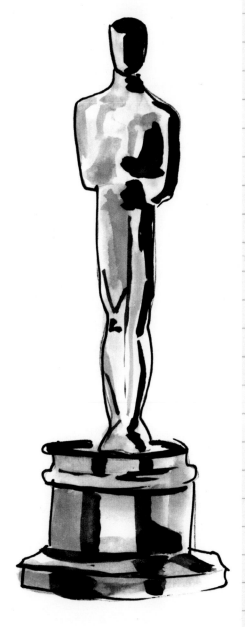

Photo Credits

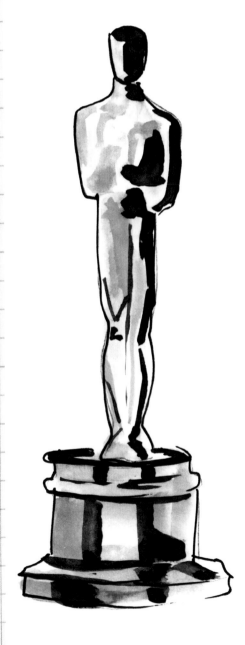

@LK Bennett

Page 87 The Gloves @ Cornelia James The Hats @Simon Tomkinson

Page 88 Daniella Helayel @Philippe Kliot @Issa

Page 91 June Kenton @Rigby & Peller

Page 92 Jane Winkworth @Dave Benett/Getty Images @French Sole

Page 94 Rachel Trevor Morgan @Rachel Trevor Morgan

Page 96 Genevieve Lawson @Cornelia James

Page 98 Harry Collins @G Collins & Sons

CHAPTER 6

Page 102 Tiffany @OIC/Xclusive G Collins & Sons @G Collins & Sons Mouawad @ Mouawad Monica Vinader @Monica Vinader

Page 103 Kiki McDonough @Kiki McDonough Asprey @Asprey Mappin & Webb @Mappin &Webb Lola Rose @Lola Rose Kristin Magnusson @ Kristin Magnusson Cartier @Cartier Merci Maman @Merci Maman

Page 104 Monica Vinader @Monica Vinader Cartier @Cartier Cassandra Goad @Cassandra Goad Pippa Small @Pippa Small Vinnie Day @Vinnie Day Kiki McDonough @Kiki McDonough Beaut's Vintage @ Beaut's Vintage CZ by Kenneth Lane @CZ by Kenneth Lane Asprey @Asprey Links of London @ Links of London Balenciaga @Balenciaga

Page 105 Catherine Zoraida @Catherine Zoraida Kiki McDonough @Kiki McDonough Mirabelle @Mirabelle Robinson Pelham @ Robinson Pelham Mappin & Webb @Mappin & Webb Links of London @Links of London Patrick Mavros @Patrick Mavros Tiffany @ Tiffany Robinson Pelham @Nunn Syndication/

Photo Credits

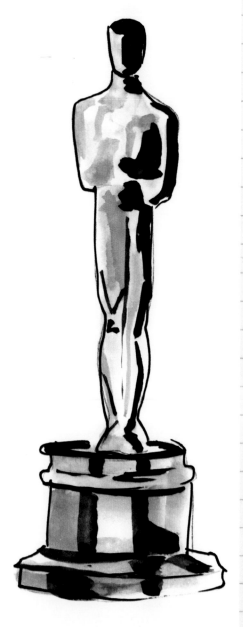

Polaris G Collins & Sons @G Collins & Sons Amrapali @ Amrapali Annoushka @ Annoushka Oscar de la Renta @Oscar de la Renta Soru Jewellery @Soru Jewellery

Page 106 Garrard @Garrard Wartski @Wartski Annoushka @Annoushka Tissot @Tissot Cartier @Cartier

Page 107 Tiffany @Tiffany Mouawad @ Mouawad Catherine Zoraida @Catherine Zoraida

CHAPTER 7

Page 110 Alexander McQueen @PA

Page 111 Beulah @Beulah

Page 112 Charlotte Todd @PA

Page 113 Diane von Furstenberg @DVF

Page 114 Erdem @mytheresa.com

Page 115 French Sole @French Sole

Page 116 G Collins & Sons @G Collins & Sons

Page 117 Hobbs @Ewa/Social Beautify

Page 118 Issa @Issa

Page 119 Jigsaw @Jigsaw

Page 120 Kiki McDonough @Kiki McDonough

Page 121 LK Bennett @LK Bennett

Page 122 Moloh @Moloh

Page 123 Nike @Nike

Page 124 Orla Kiely @Orla Kiely

Page 125 Peter Jones @Claudia Joseph

Page 127 Reiss @Reiss

Page 128 Seraphine @Seraphine

Page 129 Top Shop @Top Shop

Page 131 Vivien Sheriff @Vivien Sheriff

Page 132 Whistles @Asos

Page 133 Xmas @Alison Jackson

Page 134 YSL @YSL

Page 135 Zara @Zara

Back Cover Black Magic: @OIC/Xclusive

Acknowledgements

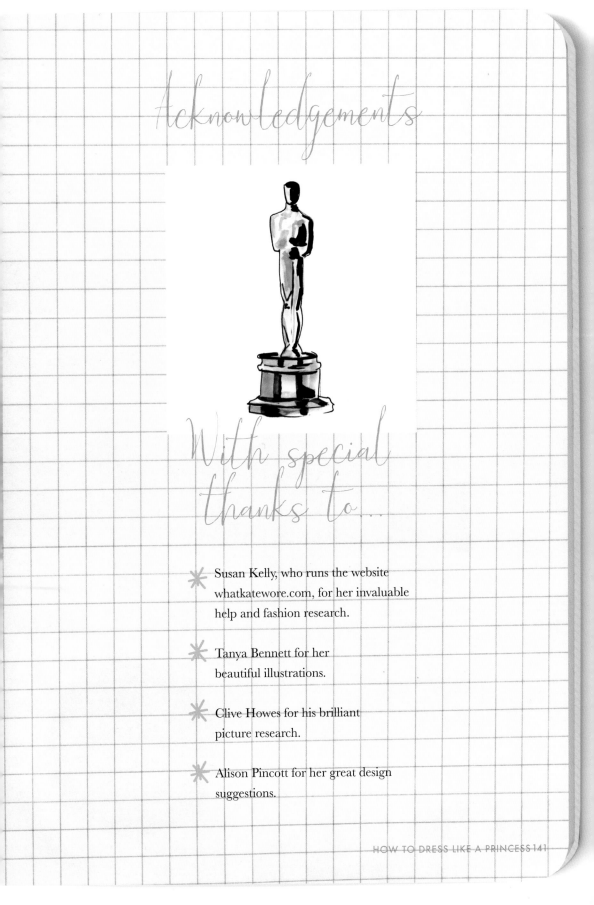

With special thanks to...

✳ Susan Kelly, who runs the website whatkatewore.com, for her invaluable help and fashion research.

✳ Tanya Bennett for her beautiful illustrations.

✳ Clive Howes for his brilliant picture research.

✳ Alison Pincott for her great design suggestions.

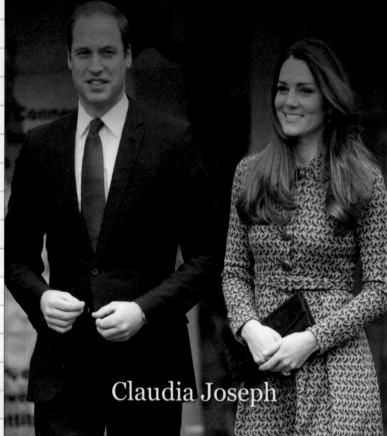

WILLIAM AND KATE'S
BRITAIN

An Insider's Guide to the haunts of the Duke and Duchess of Cambridge

Claudia Joseph